Confessions of a Confused Virgin

Where did sex come from and where is it going?

Chandler Klebs

I0416102

Table of Contents

Preface

As a young, single Christian virgin in my twenties, I started to think about girls, dating, sex, marriage, pregnancy, and babies. However, I tried to hide my thoughts and feelings for fear that people would call me a dirty, sinful pervert. I started to hate myself more and more for thinking about these things. They were not something that many Christians wanted to talk about. I prayed constantly, begging God to remove these thoughts from me, and then when he never did, I became angry at God and wanted to kill myself. Even if I killed myself, I was afraid of going to either hell or afraid that I would go to heaven and be near the God I hated. Now I can see how messed up my thoughts were. I don't hate myself or God anymore, but it has been a long process. At the time, I didn't know these thoughts were something everyone thinks about. I also heard people discuss them frequently in church during that time.

I never wanted to write a book about sex, but anyone who knows me personally knows how terribly honest I am and that no matter what they ask me, they get a short answer from me that they won't hear anywhere else.

I've written about many subjects on my blog and spoken about things in my videos on my YouTube channel. Still, after a lot of thinking, I could no longer ignore that sex was involved in everything I had ever read, from the Bible, newspapers, the internet, and even in every conversation I hear when I am around people. I was afraid to talk about it to anyone except my mom. I can't stay silent about it anymore because I think that a lot of people are confused about sex. If you're one of them, don't feel bad, because I don't even know what sex is! That, however, will not stop me from writing about it. It never stopped other Christians from writing bad books. They usually tell people that sex is evil and a "sin of the flesh". I read a terrible book once that told men not to look at women at all and to bounce their eyes away when they start to. That advice is not based on the Bible, and it is terribly rude to ignore women and leave them confused about why. I felt that I needed to write this book because maybe I'm the only one who can.

I wrote this book because I was confused about sex and marriage by preachers long before I had a clue what either was. I've learned that God did not design humans with bodies built for sex and then command them to ignore it. I don't want other young men like me to think that they can't be straight and Christian at the same time. Following the life of Jesus is a good goal, but Jesus never married. In his case, Jesus knew his purpose in life, and it didn't include marriage. Can you imagine that if he had a wife and kids, how upset they would be when he died on the cross? For him, marriage wasn't an option, but for regular men like me, it just may be.

Introduction

This book is not intended to give you any serious advice about sex. It is not a religious book intended to convert you to my beliefs. I can promise you that is not the case because my theories about sex and faith in God change on a daily basis and are influenced by how much caffeine is in my body. If you want to know how to have sex, look for another book, but if you want a good laugh, I think you'll enjoy this. I mention God and the Bible a lot because this book explains what is wrong with how many Christians view sex, dating, and marriage. It's based on what I have actually heard people say. The mention of God or religion is something that I have a hard time avoiding because it has become such a part of me that I can't ignore.

Whether you believe in God or not, he gave you a brain and a choice. I do not think that he has some eternal punishment in store for you if you happen to lust after a girl's face or have sex with the wrong person. I used to fear that God would punish me for even thinking about sex or looking at a woman's face, but now I think God is too nice for that. It is you who must decide your future. You must take responsibility for your own choices instead of blaming God, the devil, or other people.

At the time I first wrote this book, it was written from the perspective of heterosexuality, as I was taught in church and from reading the Bible. However, I have since come to see that not everyone was made for a straight marriage. I don't want to exclude anyone who is LGBTQIA+. Because I am transgender and asexual, I have come to look at this book as a history of what I used to think. I now see the evolution of my thoughts and beliefs over the years.

Chapters 1 through 8 have remained unchanged since the original 2013 publication. Chapters 9 and 10 share a few modern insights I have had in recent years.

Chapter 1: Admitting the truth

When I was much younger, I had never heard of sex. If I remember correctly, I knew about pregnancy and about babies being born. At the time though, I didn't know what caused the process to start. I just assumed women randomly got pregnant for no reason. As the years passed, my mom tried to explain sex to me and I read some books about it, but somehow words just don't help me understand something. It's all another language that I don't understand any more than Spanish. I learned to play video games by just pressing buttons on the NES controller before I could even read or understand most English spoken words. I suppose someone could learn sex by trial and error also, but what really has kept me confused is that growing up, listening to people in the various churches we attended, I was taught that you are not supposed to do sex until you are married. Then that leads to another unanswered question of mine. What is marriage? I became more and more confused as the years went by. Now as an adult, I have all these thoughts that go through my head but I never have admitted them to anyone until now. I was still afraid of what people would think of me if they knew that I thought about sex, dating, and marriage and dared to question the common "Christian" teachings.

Now I no longer go to any tax exempt, government approved "church". I am not around any religious people and it makes me feel that now is the time to tell people the truth. And the truth is, I have absolutely no idea what I'm talking about!!

Chapter 2: Where did sex come from?

I've heard and read enough to know that sex is something that two people do and that it causes women to get pregnant and babies to be born. Sadly, many people don't even say that. They say that they "have sex" when they really mean they "do sex". I could be wrong, but I think it's a verb and not a noun. So, at least, I know that it's something people do, but where did it come from? Who started it? Why does it keep going? Is it right or wrong? Will it continue forever or is it a phase that humanity will grow out of?

Genesis 1:26-28 and 2:18-24 are what most Christians would point to in the Bible to explain the origin of God creating humans as male and female and telling them to "Be fruitful and multiply". They definitely obeyed God's command to multiply or all the humans living now wouldn't be here.

So, according to the Bible, which many Christians believe is the "infallible word of God", we can learn that it was God's will for people to do sex and produce lots of babies. Why, then, do too many Christians today think that sex is a terrible sin beyond God's forgiveness? Some have invented a double standard and say that sex before marriage is a sin but if you're married to someone, then it's ok to do sex with them.

Notice carefully when you read Genesis, that the woman was called the wife of the man but it never mentioned God giving them a marriage license. The first marriage was illegal according to American standards, but the United States of America didn't exist back then and God was the only government to decide who was married!

At the moment, that's the best explanation that a virgin like me can find to explain the origin of sex. I'm not writing this to tell you to do sex but I know that you'll probably do it anyway and I don't want you to feel guilty about it or that God is angry at you.

If you happen to be one of those Atheists who don't even think there is a God, I have some simple questions for you to ask yourself. Don't you want to believe in a God who tells you that sex is okay? Have you given up on God because Christians have told you that he is mean, angry, and doesn't want you to dance, hear music, or do sex? Have you considered other options besides assuming that God doesn't exist? Only you can answer these questions, but I hope you enjoy my book whether you believe in God or not.

Chapter 3: Is sex right or wrong?

Even though we have some good evidence that sex was God's idea, there are many people who don't believe in God, and even some who are fine with God but still think sex is a bad idea.

For example, there was a group called the Shakers. They followed the teachings of Ann Lee. She didn't like sex and taught others to avoid it. As a result the group died out because they didn't have kids. This shows an important point though. Religion, just like everything else about the human race, is only kept alive because people produce kids and then teach them to believe and act the same as them.

Imagine if what happened to the Shakers happened globally to all humans. If, right now, we could get everyone to agree to stop sexing, then no one would be born and then all of humanity would die out in about 120 years. Imagine it: the end of hunger, poverty, war, etc. At least for the humans. The animals would probably still go on living without the humans polluting their homes. The idea of the end of human life on earth is such a nice thought, but it's unlikely to happen, especially after I just told people God wants them to do sex.

But there is a new thing that goes on in some Christian groups. People have "kissed dating goodbye" and the women are being taught that Jesus is their boyfriend or husband. The few Christian men that remain are being taught not to "lust" for the women. Could it be that Christians have come up with new teachings which go against, not only the Bible they claim to believe, but also against their own biology and brain? Many men, like myself, have lost hope at finding a Christian wife because we don't want to try to compete with Jesus if these women think that he is their personal romantic partner.

I believe with all my heart that something is wrong with modern Christianity and that any positive feelings that were ever involved in sex, dating, or marriage have, somehow, been lost. I know this because I have been in churches who actually teach this stuff. These are not the only reasons I was forced to leave behind traditional religion, but it's enough of a reason by itself. I've been burned badly by false religion and I hope to help others avoid it.

When I say false religion, I mean that the things people believe are false. I'm not saying that there is one "right" religion but that all systems of belief have their strengths and weaknesses and contain some things that are true and others that are false.

Chapter 4: Are sex, marriage, and love related at all?

People often have trouble defining exactly what sex, love, or marriage actually mean. People are taught that God loves them, but in this modern American life, people use the words "sex" and "love" as if they are the same thing. Somehow, I don't think they always come together. If everyone who did sex with someone loved them half as much as God loves us, I don't think there would be any break-ups or divorce. Also, love can't be sex because as far as I know, God is not literally doing anything sexual with me or anyone I know. For now, I am convinced that although marriage and sex probably would be better with love, most of the time there is no connection.

After you get past the confusion about love and sex, you still need to define marriage. Does marriage start when people do sex? Does it start when people have a fancy ceremony in a church building? Does it start when people get a marriage license from the government of the country they live in? Does it start when two people make a life-long promise to live together and help each other the rest of their lives? Different people may have these different ideas concerning marriage. Maybe your marriage might include all of these things but are these things elements of marriage or is marriage something that is far more powerful than all of these combined? These are questions I ask myself as I consider whether I should ever marry someone.

It's a bit of a fantasy to even think that somebody would want to marry a strange, autistic, computer and geometry geek who writes and speaks about religion and sex, but there are a lot of people in this world. Maybe there is someone that crazy. Right now it remains a dream. Somehow I hope that God will lead me in that direction when I am ready.

Chapter 5: Bad Dating Advice

There is very little good advice out there for Christians who want to date and find a spouse. Why is this? I think it is because so many Christians tend to think of the Bible as some kind of instruction manual. It does not contain information on potty training your children, computer programming languages, where to buy the best chicken, and many other common things people need to know. Most of all, there is no information about how to date or marry someone. Back in the Bible days, men just saw women and raped them whenever they wanted. If there was any kind of legal marriage, it was something arranged by the father of the bride. Women had no choice in what man they married. This is completely wrong. I don't believe that is God's will and was not something God gave his permission for.

Women have a few more choices living in America and in some other countries where there are laws preventing men from abusing women in the same way. Instead of women passively just accepting whatever someone else decides, they can now decide whether to stay single or to look for a husband themselves. I think women need to be more active in deciding their own future.

Advice for the women:

I have some advice for women silly enough to look for a boyfriend or husband. But you must remember that this advice comes from me as a single man. If following my advice keeps you single the rest of your life, please don't blame me. You have been warned!

First, you must know yourself and what is important to you.

If you don't know what your life is about, your future husband won't be able to understand you at all. When you think you are ready for some kind of relationship, you should probably start with those you already know. If you already have good friends that happen to be men, think about everything they've said to you, whether in person, on the phone, email, facebook, etc. Also, check whatever they publicly post on facebook or anywhere else online. If you listen to them long enough, you'll know what a mess they are. Consider if you could actually live with this person for the rest of your life. If not, stay single.

If, however, you know the perfect guy that you want to be around, then talk to him and ask him if he wants to do something. Think of some activity where you two will actually DO something. Going to see a movie or just eating at a restaurant doesn't really allow you to learn much about the other person. Try skating, swimming, running, board games, card games, video games, sports or going to the library and looking at books together. If you get hungry after doing this, though, then going together to eat something would make perfect sense. Once you have a date, below are some tips to help you better know what kind of person this man is:

Ask them Questions

Be careful not to reveal too much about your religious or political beliefs. You need to ask them questions about things to see where they stand on an issue. Start controversial topics like abortion, gay marriage, computer operating systems, the Bible, free will versus calvinism/determinism, movies, and Coke versus Pepsi. If you do this before they know what you believe, then they cannot lie and pretend to agree with you. That was what my ex-father did to fool my mom. I wish to spare you the experience of the painful marriage and divorce that I had to witness. If at any time, a big fight starts while you're talking about things, then stop dating that person immediately. It's not about who is right or wrong, but if you or your date start getting angry and fighting over things now, it will only continue.

Beat them at their own games

Find out what board games, card games, video games, or sports that a man likes. If possible, try to practice whatever game he plays and then play it with him regularly until you can win. You want to make sure that he's not too competitive or has a problem with women knowing more or playing better than him. Some people get their entire self-esteem out of how well they do at things. If he gets mad or annoyed that you can win over him, it either means he has terribly low self-esteem or he's a control freak and wants things his way all the time. Normally, you'll both just have a lot of fun and laugh no matter what happens.

Make yourself as ugly as possible

All the traditional advice from magazines or television commercials or from the internet on how to be beautiful usually include things like make-up, hair dye, dresses, etc. You should probably already be avoiding this advice because they are just money-making scams. You want to make sure that a man likes you for reasons other than your body. Try to wear big t-shirts and sweat pants. If the weather is too hot for pants then you should wear shorts. It is even better if you don't shave your legs. This way it will take a lot longer for them to be sure if you are a man or woman. Something else about your personality will be the first thing they will notice. Don't feel bad if you do not succeed in being ugly enough. It's very difficult for people to be ugly because, in reality, there is no such thing. We are all descendants of the original humans God made out of dirt. Also, each human has their own standard of beauty. Ugly is in the eye of the beholder.

Eat like you're enjoying your food

One of the biggest mistakes women make is that when eating in public, they eat very slowly and neatly. They don't want other people to know how much they eat and often don't finish their food. Eat the foods you like the best, no matter how messy they are. Eat like no one is watching. Women who are worried about eating too much or gaining weight could under-nourish their children while pregnant. Also, don't worry about burping or farting because it helps a man know that you are human. If they don't understand that women have a digestive system, then they are not the man for you. Eat some good sources of protein. You'll need some muscle if you want to do anything fun on your dates and you must be very strong and full of energy if you plan on raising kids with this guy.

Educate yourself

It's important for all people to keep their minds sharp and to learn new things. It's good to read books and try new activities you've never done before. Make sure that you have dreams or goals. If you want to go to college or some special school to learn the skills you need for a career, then do it.

Do not make the mistake of "playing dumb" as some women are taught to do. Some men seem to have a problem with women who are smarter or can do more than them. A real man should care about your spiritual and mental health as much as his own. If he tells you not to read books or not to go to college or not work a job then he wants to control everything about you. Get away from him before it's too late! Also, the more activities you are involved in, the longer he has to wait before the next time he sees you. This gives him time to get his own life figured out. If he's impatient, he'll just ignore you and find some girl who has no life. Women are usually taught to pretend that they are stupid and, somehow, think that this attracts men. What it actually does is that it convinces men that women really are stupid. Men are easily fooled by a good actress!

Advice for the men:

It would be unfair to give all these tips to the women and ignore the men. Most of it can be applied in the reverse direction. However, there are some very specific things I need to say to the men. You actually have a lot more power in this world than any woman does. Even though women are allowed to work jobs and vote now, most of the time they are not safe even walking somewhere by themselves because of evil men who will abuse them and see them as an easy target. In a perfect world where everyone loved each other perfectly, women would be safe. As it is, women do need a man to protect them. I now see it as the job of a man to protect his wife, children, and even complete strangers who can't defend themselves. This is not a "God given" job, in my opinion, because God never intended this world to turn into the mess that it has, but if you have any love in you at all, you will want to do this if you can.

What you must know about women is that they are people just like you. They look different but they can still think, talk, read, write, eat, drink, sleep, burp, and fart just as well as a man. They only tend to look cuter while doing everything. If there is a woman you want as a girlfriend or wife, you need to make sure that you like something about her other than her body. Not only because she won't always look the same as she does now, but also because, if you don't on some level connect mentally and understand her brain, you will, in the future, have more and more things you discover that you disagree about.

For example, one spouse believes in God and wants to follow the teachings of Jesus and the other says there is no God and no right or wrong way to live. Imagine if these people had children! They would be so confused because their parents would fight about everything. Or imagine one spouse believes in eating healthy, organic food as natural and nutritious as possible while the other just eats fast food all the time. Who decides the best way to feed the kids? This is exactly why both men and women must know everything about each other before they make any life-long commitment to each other.

As a man, I can tell other men that I completely understand that you like the body of most women you see. There is nothing wrong with this but if a female body is ALL you want, you should probably buy a female mannequin and just stare at it all you want. If you don't love women and see them as equally important as you, then do the entire world a favor and don't date any woman. It's just cruel to pretend to care about someone and then let them discover you see them only as an object to use.

One more tip, while you are looking for the right woman to date. Don't ignore women who already have kids. In a perfect world, they already would have a father, but most of the time, a woman is raising kids by herself because a man lied to her. He made promises he never intended to keep. Then, as soon as he decided he didn't love her or the children, he left the mother to struggle on her own.

How do I know this? Because that's what my ex-father did. My mother raised me by herself. It was not easy growing up the way I did and the things I had to see. I can't count how many times I asked God for a good dad who would protect my mom from the bad dad. Every time I am out in public and a child looks directly into my eyes and calls me "daddy", I go home and cry because I know that most likely, to that child, I look like a daddy, but if they had a daddy around, they would be talking to him. Where did he go?

I would do anything I could to prevent another child from living that experience. If you happen to be a man reading this, you need to carefully consider whether given the chance, would you date or marry a woman who has children? I know I would. I would gladly marry a single mother and adopt her children and love them as much as if they had been mine from the start. I don't think that a baby conceived from my sperm would be superior in any way. Obviously, the woman and her children would have to want me in their family as well. I would make sure I had permission from the children before I could make any serious decisions. Children don't often get such a choice and I think they should.

Chapter 6: What is Lust?

According to the research I have done, the word "lust" is usually defined as a strong "desire" or "craving". For some odd reason, people tend to assume that the desire or craving is always sexual whenever the word "lust" is used. Christians need to stop shouting this word at everyone when they have no clue what it actually means. It can mean many things. For example, lust for food is hunger. Lust for water is thirst. There needs to be a commonly understood word to mean the same as sexual lust. For example, the word attraction is commonly used this way.

When people finally learn what the word lust means, they understand what the Christians have been telling them. They mean "don't desire a wife" or "don't be attracted to women". This is the message that so many Christians tell the men and then wonder why the men are turning gay, which by the way, they also preach against. Words are powerful when repeated long enough. This, I believe, is how organized religion damages lives. There is nothing wrong with religion, but don't let it think for you. Only you know how you really feel. When someone tells you that your thoughts or feelings are sinful, you feel bad and try to change them but they are part of you. There is no magic switch to turn them on or off. It's useless to tell the men not to lust. They will, no matter what you say. Instead, men should be taught how to love. It's possible to love and lust at the same time. It's called multi-tasking.

Here is a question for the women: Do you want to have your boyfriend or husband tell you that he can't see you any more? Imagine if he called you and said. "I love you but I can no longer meet with you in person because if I see you, I might desire you and I can't do that because then I would be living in sin. We can have a long-distance relationship by phone and email, but I cannot look at you because you're much too attractive."

Think about that. Does that make you feel loved? Maybe now you can see why a little lust can make a better marriage.

Chapter 7: What is pornography?

People are unable to define words like sex, dating, marriage, and lust. There is another word that people tend to use which still confuses me. The word "pornography" is a very vague word just like the others. What do you think of as soon as you see that word? In the past, I assumed that any time something contained a naked woman, it was to be called pornography. Therefore, since women's faces are naked, they must be a form of pornography. By that definition, it's impossible to avoid it. Some people would think that is silly but I actually thought that. I think that unless people can define what it is, it's very hard to fight against. Because of this confusion, I would like to tell you exactly how I define "pornography".

I think that pornography is when people use any form of a human body, whether male or female, and try to use it to cheat people out of their money by lying to them that they need to buy their products in order to experience a type of sex that God never created.

The first type of pornography I will mention is the kind that targets women. Women, in this world, are told that the way to get men to love them is to change the appearance of their body. Greedy people make a lot of money off of women by selling them hair dye, make-up, fingernail polish, earrings, jewellery, over-priced clothes which contain very little material, and weight loss products. Somehow, people think that the ideal woman is skinny, weak, blonde, painted, naked, silent, and stupid. I think it's sad that so many women are falling for this lie. There are a lot of people who will lose a lot of money if women find out the truth. That is why I must tell you, women, that you don't need any of these things. If God had intended you to look that way, you already would. You can't make men love you no matter how much money you spend. Love comes from God and men will love you only when they have learned that God loves them and that they should love all people.

The second, and most common form of pornography, is that which targets men. Anything that a company wants to sell such as a car, computer, video game, book, magazine, swimming pool, or anything else, all they need to do is advertise with some pictures or videos of naked women. It must be working because they keep doing it. Men are easily fooled, too, but in a different way. Men are made to feel bad when religious people tell them that looking at pornography is a sin. Because looking at women makes them feel good, they still do it but try to keep it a secret. With television, the internet, and newspapers, it's easy to see all the women they want. The worst part is that the type of women they see are not even real! Men have no practice at even talking to women because they have spent so much time looking at pictures of women in magazines or websites that don't talk to them. Men need to know that women talk. They talk a lot! Also, they don't even have a clue what women really look like because so often these images have been altered with all kinds of computer software.

Men have such false ideas of what a woman is, even if they have a wife, they don't know what to do with her because they haven't figured out she's a person!

Men and women need to stop judging each other and realize that they are both more than bodies and, instead of fighting, they should use their differences to help each other. Both men and women have been lied to about many things.

Chapter 8: Where is sex going?

I know that humans will continue doing sex and producing more children. The only question is whether or not there will be any true families. Will men and women finally be treated equally? Will they get along? I hope that such things as fighting, abuse, divorce, abortion, and all the shame surrounding sex will eventually be completely gone. My main goal in writing this is to educate people so that all people can work together to resolve the problems that are going on everywhere all over the world.

Here is the future I would create if I had the power:

People will do sex, but they will only do it of their own will with those they love. All children will be wanted and there will be no abortion. All children will have two parents who do what is best for them. All forms of pornography will completely be shut down simply because people are no longer fooled and will never spend money on such things. All people will be treated as equally important no matter what their age, race, gender, religion, or anything else. That is the type of world I want. I hope that others will help me work toward it.

If there is a subject I didn't cover that you were hoping for or things I could explain better, please email me at

chandlerklebs@gmail.com

Your comments, suggestions, and experiences with this may help me expose the lies about sex even better.

Chapter 9: I'm Still Confused and Still a Virgin

Originally I wrote this book in 2013 while I was trying to figure out many things related to Christianity and sexuality. Since then two major changes have happened.

1. I'm no longer a traditional Christian by any stretch of the imagination. I found too many contradictions in the religion I was raised in and slowly lost the idea that there even was such a thing as a true Christian or right religion. I see religion as a scam to make money off of people. It's well known to people who have read my later books or seen my other online work that I no longer believe in the Christian God (as presented by American Christianity).

2. I now identify as asexual. That is, I discovered that I have either no sexual desire or it's so low as to not affect me. I used to think that I was straight because I once liked the idea of marrying a woman and having children like most normal people. However that was done in the context that it was God's will for me to do that. I hadn't even questioned whether it was something that I wanted. I now have other priorities. Since I would rather be watching My Little Pony, recording podcasts, or playing video games, I have no use for the concepts of sex or marriage.

I know this may come as a shock to people who knew me in the past or have read this book. That's why I am updating it. I want to cover a brief history of what happened to change my views.

The most major change was when I started working at Hy-Vee in October of 2012. It was the biggest major social change in my life. Instead of going to church for all my social interaction, I was sacking groceries and bringing in carts. I started liking the people I was around.

However I had other emotional conflicts going on in my head. My head was filled with all kinds of messages from Christianity. I wasn't sure back then what I believed and I wondered whether I was going to heaven or hell when I died. I was rather selfish during that time. I was trying to make sense out of the bible and reading other books about Christianity. I wanted to make sure I believed and/or did the right things to avoid going to hell.

But then something else happened. I began to think about OTHER people and their eternal destiny. So I set out to find the truth about God, Jesus, heaven, hell, and other things. I listened to a man named Joshua Tongol. He convinced me that God was nice. I believed that for a few months, but then I later saw that everything I believed was just what other people told me. I had no evidence or experience to keep me believing in a good god that was powerful enough to wipe out evil but didn't want to.

The problem of evil continued to eat away at my former beliefs. I was increasingly upset about the abortion issue. I spent two years talking to people online about abortion and reading all kinds of arguments back and forth about why people should or should not kill their babies.

As you can imagine, I became extremely upset about the aborted babies. However then it led to another huge life change. I went vegetarian after I started seeing other animals as being equal to humans. I had been taught all my life that God gave humans permission to kill animals and that humans were more valuable for being made in the image of God(whatever that means). But none of that mattered. Other animals were suffering in factory farms. They were being tortured and killed in ways that no human would want done to themselves!

So as my knowledge of the cruel things humans were doing grew, so did my pessimism. I wanted to know what was wrong with everybody! I found quite a few errors in my own thinking along the way. I've become aware of my emotional biases that led me to believe things based on what I would like to believe is true.

All that's really left is my desire to be happy and to reduce the pain in the world. It's for this reason that I follow a life of non-violence as much as I know how. I'm a Vegan because I don't want to buy food that was obtained though violence to animals. Most of all I see eating beef, chicken, turkey, or pork to be just like eating human meat. It makes me sick if I think about it too much.

I see the ugly realities of this world and I'm in a never ending process of trying to do what I think will help reduce it. This all relates to what I think of sexuality.

I now no longer think sex is ever a good idea. It's not worth the risk. The two most common problems with sexuality are Sexually Transmitted Diseases and unwanted pregnancy.

But suppose that people do intend to reproduce and that's why they are having sex. There are problems with this too. When people have kids, they don't know whether or not they will be happy. They also don't know what those children will do during their entire lifetime. Basically it's a gamble. Most likely their children will suffer by the actions of others and will also cause suffering to others.

Ironically, I do see that this conflicts with my other feelings about abortion. I'm against killing the unborn but at the same time, I'd rather they not be conceived in the first place. There are already children who need to be adopted. Why create more?

So those are my views right now. I'm asexual but also anti-sexual because of the harm of reproduction and risk of diseases. So I will be a confused virgin for life.

I learned one thing though that is very important. How I feel about this or what I write is not likely to change what other people do. The main purpose of this is to help explain some of the extreme changes that happened since I first published this book in May of 2013. It's still a very funny read and I hope that you enjoyed it.

Chapter 10: What the Hell did I write?!

On May 15, 2025, I had my 38th birthday. After publishing my latest book, *Chastity's Chess Chapters*, I decided I should use my markdown skills to preserve some of my older writing in a plain text form that I can always read, share, and update.

But when I stumbled upon *Confessions of a Confused Virgin*, I was surprised both by how much and how little had changed since November of 2013 when I first wrote and published this book.

The one thing that has not changed is that I am still a confused virgin. In fact, I call myself the Vegan Virgin because men are shamed for being virgins, and they are considered not men unless they have had sex. Therefore, if I never have sex, I am a woman! I have reclaimed being a Virgin as a badge of honor and connected it with my Vegan ethics of doing no harm to animals!

For a minute, because I no longer agree with a lot of what I wrote in this book, I had considered deleting this book from the internet, but then I remembered that it was this very poorly written book that was a stepping stone for me to learn about self-publishing. Since this book was published, I have published many newer books.

Therefore, consider the book you just read as a history of what I thought back in 2013. For my more recent thoughts on sexuality, *The Vow of Chastity* is the best reference. For more information on what happened to me during my gender journey from a man named Chandler to a

Transgender Woman named Chastity, read the *Chandler's Honesty* series.

Chastity's Book List

The following is a list of all my books in the order they were published.

- Confessions of a Confused Virgin
- Irrelevant
- Free Will and Abortion Denial
- The Anti-Abortion Atheistic Animal
- Determinism Vs Indeterminism
- The Vow of Chastity
- Chandler's Honesty (series of books)
- Chastity's Chess Chapters
- Who is the Sinner?

You can usually find these and my future books by visiting

https://books2read.com/ap/nlZV3A/Chastity-White-Rose

Paperbacks and Kindle editions can also be found on Amazon. You may have to try searching for "Chandler Klebs" to find my older books and "Chastity White Rose" for my newer books.

Contact information

My email address that I created when I chose my new name is:

chastitywhiterose@gmail.com

Contact me if you want to talk or want more information about what I do. I am on most social media too although I don't often use them for much besides posting my latest writing or chess videos.

https://www.linkedin.com/in/chastity-rose-96aaa492/

https://linktr.ee/chastitywhiterose

https://www.instagram.com/chastitywhiterose/

https://twitter.com/Chastity_W_Rose

https://chastitywhiterose.com/

https://chastitychesschallenge.com/